Second State of the Union Address

JAMES KNOX POLK

1846

TABLE OF CONTENTS

FELLOW-CITIZENS OF THE SENATE AND OF THE HOUSE OF REPRESENTATIVES

In resuming your labors in the service of the people it is a subject of congratulation that there has been no period in our past history when all the elements of national prosperity have been so fully developed. Since your last session no afflicting dispensation has visited our country. General good health has prevailed, abundance has crowned the toil of the husbandman, and labor in all its branches is receiving an ample reward, while education, science, and the arts are rapidly enlarging the means of social happiness. The progress of our country in her career of greatness, not only in the vast extension of our territorial limits and the rapid increase of our population, but in resources and wealth and in the happy condition of our people, is without an example in the history of nations.

As the wisdom, strength, and beneficence of our free institutions are unfolded, every day adds fresh motives to contentment and fresh incentives to patriotism.

Our devout and sincere acknowledgments are due to the gracious Giver of All Good for the numberless blessings which our beloved country enjoys.

It is a source of high satisfaction to know that the relations of the United States with all other nations, with a single exception, are of the most amicable character. Sincerely attached to the policy of peace early adopted and steadily pursued by this Government, I have anxiously desired to cultivate and cherish friendship and commerce with every foreign power.

The spirit and habits of the American people are favorable to the maintenance of such international harmony. In adhering to this wise policy, a preliminary and paramount duty obviously consists in the protection of our national interests from encroachment or sacrifice and our national honor from reproach. These must be maintained at any hazard. They admit of no compromise or neglect, and must be scrupulously and constantly guarded. In their vigilant vindication collision and conflict with foreign powers may sometimes become unavoidable. Such has been our scrupulous adherence to the dictates of justice in all our foreign intercourse that, though steadily and rapidly advancing in prosperity and power, we have given no just cause of complaint to any nation and have enjoyed the blessings of peace for more than thirty years. From a policy so sacred to humanity and so salutary in its effects upon our political system we should never be induced voluntarily to depart.

The existing war with Mexico was neither desired nor provoked by the United States. On the contrary, all honorable means were resorted to to avert it. After years of endurance of aggravated and unredressed wrongs on our part, Mexico, in violation of solemn treaty stipulations and of every principle of justice recognized by civilized nations, commenced hostilities, and thus by her own act forced the war upon us. Long before the advance of our Army to the left bank of the Rio Grande we had ample cause of war against Mexico, and had the United States resorted to this extremity we might have appealed to the whole civilized world for the justice of our cause. I deem it to be my duty to present to you on the present occasion a condensed review of the injuries we had sustained, of the causes which led to the war, and of its progress since its commencement. This is rendered the more necessary because of the misapprehensions which have to some extent prevailed as to its origin and true character. The war has been represented as unjust and unnecessary and as one of aggression on our part upon a weak and injured enemy. Such erroneous views, though entertained by but few, have been widely and extensively circulated, not only at home, but have been spread throughout Mexico and the whole world. A more effectual means could not have been devised to encourage the enemy and protract the war than to advocate and adhere to their cause, and thus give them "aid and comfort." It is a source of national pride and exultation that the great body of our people have thrown no such obstacles in the way of the Government in prosecuting the war successfully, but have shown themselves to be eminently patriotic and ready to vindicate their country's honor and interests at any sacrifice. The alacrity and promptness with which our volunteer forces rushed to the field on their country's call prove not only their patriotism, but their deep conviction that our cause is just.

The wrongs which we have suffered from Mexico almost ever since she became an independent power and the patient endurance with which we have borne them are without a parallel in the history of modern civilized nations. There is reason to believe that if these wrongs had been resented and resisted in the first instance the present war might have been avoided. One outrage, however, permitted to pass with impunity almost necessarily encouraged the perpetration of another, until at last Mexico seemed to attribute to weakness and indecision on our part a forbearance which was the offspring of magnanimity and of a sincere desire to preserve friendly relations with a sister republic.

Scarcely had Mexico achieved her independence, which the United States were the first among the nations to acknowledge, when she commenced the system of insult and spoliation which she has ever since pursued. Our citizens engaged in lawful commerce were imprisoned, their vessels seized, and our flag insulted in her ports. If money was wanted, the lawless seizure and confiscation of our merchant vessels and their cargoes was a ready resource, and if to accomplish their purposes it became necessary to imprison the owners, captains, and crews, it was done. Rulers superseded rulers in Mexico in rapid succession, but still there was no change in this system of depredation. The Government of the United States made repeated reclamations on behalf of its citizens, but these were answered by the perpetration of new outrages. Promises of redress made by Mexico in the most solemn forms were postponed or evaded. The files and records of the Department of State contain conclusive proofs of numerous lawless acts perpetrated upon the property and persons of our citizens by Mexico, and of wanton insults to our national flag. The interposition of our Government to obtain redress was again and again invoked under circumstances which no nation ought to disregard. It was hoped that these outrages would cease and that Mexico would be restrained by the laws which regulate the conduct of civilized nations in their intercourse with each other after the treaty of amity, commerce, and navigation of the 5th of April, 1831, was concluded between the two Republics; but this hope soon proved to be vain. The course of seizure and confiscation of the property of our citizens, the violation of their persons, and the insults to our flag pursued by Mexico previous to that time were scarcely suspended for even a brief period, although the treaty so clearly defines the rights and duties of the respective parties that it is impossible to misunderstand or mistake them. In less than seven years after the conclusion of that treaty our grievances had become so intolerable that in the opinion of President Jackson they should no longer be endured. In his message to Congress in February, 1837, he presented them to the consideration of that body, and declared that-

The length of time since some of the injuries have been committed, the repeated and unavailing applications for redress, the wanton character of some of the outrages upon the property and persons of our citizens, upon the officers and flag of the United States, independent of recent insults to this Government and people by the late extraordinary Mexican minister, would justify in the eyes of all nations immediate war.

In a spirit of kindness and forbearance, however, he recommended reprisals as a milder mode of redress. He declared that war should not be used as a remedy "by just and generous nations, confiding in their strength for injuries committed, if it can be honorably avoided," and added:

It has occurred to me that, considering the present embarrassed condition of that country, we should act with both wisdom and moderation by giving to Mexico one more opportunity to atone for the past before we take redress into our Own hands. To avoid all misconception on the part of Mexico, as well as to protect our own national character from reproach, this opportunity should be given with the avowed design and full preparation to take immediate satisfaction if it should not be obtained on a repetition of the demand for it. To this end I recommend that an act be passed authorizing reprisals, and the use of the naval force of the United States by the Executive against Mexico to enforce them, in the event of a refusal by the Mexican Government to come to an amicable adjustment of the matters in controversy between us upon another demand thereof made from on board out of our vessels of war on the coast of Mexico.

Committees of both Houses of Congress, to which this message of the President was referred, fully sustained his views of the character of the wrongs which we had suffered from Mexico, and recommended that another demand for redress should be made before authorizing war or reprisals. The Committee on Foreign Relations of the Senate, in their report, say:

After such a demand, should prompt justice be refused by the Mexican Government, we may appeal to all nations, not only for the equity and moderation with which we shall have acted toward a sister republic, but for the necessity which will then compel us to seek redress for our wrongs, either by actual war or by reprisals. The subject will then be presented before Congress, at the commencement of the next session, in a clear and distinct form, and the committee can not doubt but that such measures will be immediately adopted as may be necessary to vindicate the honor of the country and insure ample reparation to our injured fellow-citizens.

The Committee on Foreign Affairs of the House of Representatives made a similar recommendation. In their report they say that-

They fully concur with the President that ample cause exists for taking redress into our own hands, and believe that we should be justified in the opinion of other nations for taking such a step. But they are willing to try the experiment of another demand, made in the most solemn form, upon the justice of the Mexican Government before any further proceedings are adopted.

No difference of opinion upon the subject is believed to have existed in Congress at that time; the executive and legislative departments concurred; and yet such has been our forbearance and desire to preserve peace with Mexico that the wrongs of which we then complained, and which gave rise to these solemn proceedings, not only remain unredressed to this day, but additional causes of complaint of an aggravated character have ever since been accumulating. Shortly after these proceedings a special messenger was dispatched to Mexico to make a final demand for redress, and on the 20th of July, 1837, the demand was made. The reply of the Mexican Government bears date on the 29th of the same month, and contains assurances of the "anxious wish" of the Mexican Government "not to delay the moment of that final and equitable adjustment which is to terminate the existing difficulties between the two Governments;" that "nothing should be left undone which may contribute to the most speedy and equitable determination of the subjects which have so seriously engaged the attention of the American Government;" that the "Mexican Government would adopt as the only guides for its conduct the plainest principles of public right, the sacred obligations imposed by international law, and the religious faith of treaties," and that "whatever reason and justice may dictate respecting each case will be done." The assurance was further given that the decision of the Mexican Government upon each cause of complaint for which redress had been demanded should be communicated to the Government of the United States by the Mexican minister at Washington.

These solemn assurances in answer to our demand for redress were disregarded. By making them, however, Mexico obtained further delay. President Van Buren, in his annual message to Congress of the 5th of December, 1837, states that "although the larger number" of our demands for redress, "and many of them aggravated cases of personal wrongs, have been now for years before the Mexican Government, and some of the causes of national complaint, and those of the most offensive character, admitted of immediate, simple, and satisfactory replies, it is only within a few days past that any specific communication in answer to our last demand, made five months ago, has been received from the Mexican minister;" and that "for not one of our public complaints has satisfaction been given or offered, that but one of the cases of personal wrong has been favorably considered, and that but four cases of both descriptions out of all those formally presented and earnestly pressed have as yet been decided upon by the Mexican Government." President Van Buren, believing that it would be vain to make any further attempt to obtain redress by the ordinary means within the power of the Executive, communicated this opinion to Congress in the message referred to, in which he said:

On a careful and deliberate examination of their contents of the correspondence with the Mexican Government], and considering the spirit manifested by the Mexican Government, it has become my painful duty to return the subject as it now stands to Congress, to whom it belongs to decide upon the time, the mode, and the measure of redress.

Had the United States at that time adopted compulsory measures and taken redress into their own hands, all our difficulties with Mexico would probably have been long since adjusted and the existing war have been averted. Magnanimity and moderation on our part only had the effect to complicate these difficulties and render an amicable settlement of them the more embarrassing. That such measures of redress under similar provocations committed by any of the powerful nations of Europe would have been promptly resorted to by the United States can not be doubted. The national honor and the preservation of the national character throughout the world, as well as our own self-respect and the protection due to our own citizens, would have rendered such a resort indispensable. The history of no civilized nation in modern times has presented within so brief a period so many wanton attacks upon the honor of its flag and upon the property and persons of its citizens as had at that time been borne by the United States from the Mexican authorities and people. But Mexico was a sister republic on the North American continent, occupying a territory contiguous to our own, and was in a feeble and distracted condition, and these considerations, it is presumed, induced Congress to forbear still longer.

Instead of taking redress into our own hands, a new negotiation was entered upon with fair promises on the part of Mexico, but with the real purpose, as the event has proved, of indefinitely postponing the reparation which we demanded, and which was so justly due. This negotiation, after more than a year's delay, resulted in the convention of the 11th of April, 1839, "for the adjustment of claims of citizens of the United States of

America upon the Government of the Mexican Republic." The joint board of commissioners created by this convention to examine and decide upon these claims was not organized until the month of August, 1840, and under the terms of the convention they were to terminate their duties within eighteen months from that time. Four of the eighteen months were consumed in preliminary discussions on frivolous and dilatory points raised by the Mexican commissioners, and it was not until the month of December, 1840, that they commenced the examination of the claims of our citizens upon Mexico. Fourteen months only remained to examine and decide upon these numerous and complicated cases. In the month of February, 1842, the term of the commission expired, leaving many claims undisposed of for want of time. The claims which were allowed by the board and by the umpire authorized by the convention to decide in case of disagreement between the Mexican and American commissioners amounted to $2,026,139.68. There were pending before the umpire when the commission expired additional claims, which had been examined and awarded by the American commissioners and had not been allowed by the Mexican commissioners, amounting to $928,627.88, upon which he did not decide, alleging that his authority had ceased with the termination of the joint commission. Besides these claims, there were others of American citizens amounting to $3,336,837.05, which had been submitted to the board, and upon which they had not time to decide before their final adjournment.

The sum of $2,026,139.68, which had been awarded to the claimants, was a liquidated and ascertained debt due by Mexico, about which there could be no dispute, and which she was bound to pay according to the terms of the convention. Soon after the final awards for this amount had been made the Mexican Government asked for a postponement of the time of making payment, alleging that it would be inconvenient to make the payment at the time stipulated. In the spirit of forbearing kindness toward a sister republic, which Mexico has so long abused, the United States promptly complied with her request. A second convention was accordingly concluded between the two Governments on the 30th of January, 1843, which upon its face declares that "this new arrangement is entered into for the accommodation of Mexico." By the terms of this convention all the interest due on the awards which had been made in favor of the claimants under the convention of the 11th of April, 1839, was to be paid to them on the 30th of April, 1843, and "the principal of the said awards and the interest accruing thereon" was stipulated to "be paid in five years, in equal installments every three months." Notwithstanding this new convention was entered into at the request of Mexico and for the purpose of relieving her from embarrassment, the claimants have only received the interest due

11

on the 30th of April, 1843, and three of the twenty installments. Although the payment of the sum thus liquidated and confessedly due by Mexico to our citizens as indemnity for acknowledged acts of outrage and wrong was secured by treaty, the obligations of which are ever held sacred by all just nations, yet Mexico has violated this solemn engagement by failing and refusing to make the payment. The two installments due in April and July, 1844, under the peculiar circumstances connected with them, have been assumed by the United States and discharged to the claimants, but they are still due by Mexico. But this is not all of which we have just cause of complaint. To provide a remedy for the claimants whose cases were not decided by the joint commission under the convention of April 11, 1839, it was expressly stipulated by the sixth article of the convention of the 30th of January, 1843, that-

A new convention shall be entered into for the settlement of all claims of the Government and citizens of the United States against the Republic of Mexico which were not finally decided by the late commission which met in the city of Washington, and of all claims of the Government and citizens of Mexico against the United States.

In conformity with this stipulation, a third convention was concluded and signed at the city of Mexico on the 20th of November, 1843, by the plenipotentiaries of the two Governments, by which provision was made for ascertaining and paying these claims. In January, 1844, this convention was ratified by the Senate of the United States with two amendments, which were manifestly reasonable in their character. Upon a reference of the amendments proposed to the Government of Mexico, the same evasions, difficulties, and delays were interposed which have so long marked the policy of that Government toward the United States. It has not even yet decided whether it would or would not accede to them, although the subject has been repeatedly pressed upon its consideration. Mexico has thus violated a second time the faith of treaties by failing or refusing to carry into effect the sixth article of the convention of January, 1843.

Such is the history of the wrongs which we have suffered and patiently endured from Mexico through a long series of years. So far from affording reasonable satisfaction for the injuries and insults we had borne, a great aggravation of them consists in the fact that while the United States, anxious to preserve a good understanding with Mexico, have been constantly but vainly employed in seeking redress for past wrongs, new outrages were constantly occurring, which have continued to increase our causes of complaint and to swell the amount of our demands. While the citizens of the United States were conducting a lawful commerce with

Mexico under the guaranty of a treaty of "amity, commerce, and navigation," many of them have suffered all the injuries which would have resulted from open war. This treaty, instead of affording protection to our citizens, has been the means of inviting them into the ports of Mexico that they might be, as they have been in numerous instances, plundered of their property and deprived of their personal liberty if they dared insist on their rights. Had the unlawful seizures of American property and the violation of the personal liberty of our citizens, to say nothing of the insults to our flag, which have occurred in the ports of Mexico taken place on the high seas, they would themselves long since have constituted a state of actual war between the two countries. In so long suffering Mexico to violate her most solemn treaty obligations, plunder our citizens of their property, and imprison their persons without affording them any redress we have failed to perform one of the first and highest duties which every government owes to its citizens, and the consequence has been that many of them have been reduced from a state of affluence to bankruptcy. The proud name of American citizen, which ought to protect all who bear it from insult and injury throughout the world, has afforded no such protection to our citizens in Mexico. We had ample cause of war against Mexico long before the breaking out of hostilities; but even then we forbore to take redress into our own hands until Mexico herself became the aggressor by invading our soil in hostile array and shedding the blood of our citizens.

Such are the grave causes of complaint on the part of the United States against Mexico-causes which existed long before the annexation of Texas to the American Union; and yet, animated by the love of peace and a magnanimous moderation, we did not adopt those measures of redress which under such circumstances are the justified resort of injured nations.

The annexation of Texas to the United States constituted no just cause of offense to Mexico. The pretext that it did so is wholly inconsistent and irreconcilable with well-authenticated facts connected with the revolution by which Texas became independent of Mexico. That this may be the more manifest, it may be proper to advert to the causes and to the history of the principal events of that revolution.

Texas constituted a portion of the ancient Province of Louisiana, ceded to the United States by France in the year 1803. In the year 1819 the United States, by the Florida treaty, ceded to Spain all that part of Louisiana within the present limits of Texas, and Mexico, by the revolution which separated her from Spain and rendered her an independent nation, succeeded to the rights of the mother country over this territory. In the year 1824 Mexico established a federal constitution, under which the Mexican Republic was composed of a number of sovereign States confederated together in a federal union similar to our own. Each of these States had its own executive, legislature, and judiciary, and for all except federal purposes was as independent of the General Government and that of the other States as is Pennsylvania or Virginia under our Constitution. Texas and Coahuila united and formed one of these Mexican States. The State constitution which they adopted, and which was approved by the Mexican Confederacy, asserted that they were "free and independent of the other Mexican United States and of every other power and dominion whatsoever," and proclaimed the great principle of human liberty that "the sovereignty of the state resides originally and essentially in the general mass of the individuals who compose it." To the Government under this constitution, as well as to that under the federal constitution, the people of Texas owed allegiance.

Emigrants from foreign countries, including the United States, were invited by the colonization laws of the State and of the Federal Government to settle in Texas. Advantageous terms were offered to induce them to leave their own country and become Mexican citizens. This invitation was accepted by many of our citizens in the full faith that in their new home they would be governed by laws enacted by representatives elected by themselves, and that their lives, liberty, and property would be protected by constitutional guaranties similar to those which existed in the Republic they had left. Under a Government thus organized they continued until the year 1835, when a military revolution broke out in the City of Mexico which entirely subverted the federal and State constitutions and placed a military dictator at the head of the Government. By a sweeping decree of a Congress subservient to the will of the Dictator the several State constitutions were abolished and the States themselves converted into mere departments of the central Government. The people of Texas were unwilling to submit to this usurpation. Resistance to such tyranny became a high duty. Texas was fully absolved from all allegiance to the central Government of Mexico from the moment that Government had abolished her State constitution and in its place substituted an arbitrary and despotic central government. Such were the principal causes of the Texan revolution. The people of Texas at once determined upon resistance and flew to arms. In the midst of these important and exciting events, however, they did not omit to place their liberties upon a secure and permanent foundation. They elected members to a convention, who in the month of March, 1836, issued a formal declaration that their "political connection with the Mexican nation has forever ended, and that the people of Texas do now constitute a free, sovereign, and independent Republic, and are fully invested with all the rights and attributes which properly belong to independent nations." They also adopted for their government a liberal republican constitution. About the same time Santa Anna, then the Dictator of Mexico, invaded Texas with a numerous army for the purpose of subduing her people and enforcing obedience to his arbitrary and despotic Government. On the 21st of April, 1836, he was met by the Texan citizen soldiers, and on that day was achieved by them the memorable victory of San Jacinto, by which they conquered their independence. Considering the numbers engaged on the respective sides, history does not record a more brilliant achievement. Santa Anna himself was among the captives.

In the month of May, 1836, Santa Anna acknowledged by a treaty with the Texan authorities in the most solumn form "the full, entire, and perfect independence of the Republic of Texas." It is true he was then a prisoner of war, but it is equally true that he had failed to reconquer Texas, and had met with signal defeat; that his authority had not been revoked, and that by virtue of this treaty he obtained his personal release. By it hostilities were suspended, and the army which had invaded Texas under his command returned in pursuance of this arrangement unmolested to Mexico.

From the day that the battle of San Jacinto was fought until the present hour Mexico has never possessed the power to reconquer Texas. In the language of the Secretary of State of the United States in a dispatch to our minister in Mexico under date of the 8th of July, 1842-

Mexico may have chosen to consider, and may still choose to consider, Texas as having been at all times since 1835, and as still continuing, a rebellious province; but the world has been obliged to take a very different view of the matter. From the time of the battle of San Jacinto, in April, 1836, to the present moment, Texas has exhibited the same external signs of national independence as Mexico herself, and with quite as much stability of government. Practically free and independent, acknowledged as a political sovereignty by the principal powers of the world, no hostile foot finding rest within her territory for six or seven years, and Mexico herself refraining for all that period from any further attempt to reestablish her own authority over that territory, it can not but be surprising to find Mr. De Bocanegra the secretary of foreign affairs of Mexico] complaining that for that whole period citizens of the United States or its Government have been favoring the rebels of Texas and supplying them with vessels, ammunition, and money, as if the war for the reduction of the Province of Texas had been constantly prosecuted by Mexico, and her success prevented by these influences from abroad.

In the same dispatch the Secretary of State affirms that- Since 1837 the United States have regarded Texas as an independent sovereignty as much as Mexico, and that trade and commerce with citizens of a government at war with Mexico can not on that account be regarded as an intercourse by which assistance and succor are given to Mexican rebels. The whole current of Mr. De Bocanegra's remarks runs in the same direction, as if the independence of Texas had not been acknowledged. It has been acknowledged; it was acknowledged in 1837 against the remonstrance and protest of Mexico, and most of the acts of any importance of which Mr. De Bocanegra complains flow necessarily from that recognition. He speaks of Texas as still being "an integral part of the territory of the Mexican Republic," but he can not but understand that the United States do not so regard it. The real complaint of Mexico, therefore, is in substance neither more nor less than a complaint against the recognition of Texan independence. It may be thought rather late to repeat that complaint, and not quite just to confine it to the United States to the exemption of England, France, and Belgium, unless the United States, having been the first to acknowledge the independence of Mexico herself, are to be blamed for setting an example for the recognition of that of Texas.

And he added that- The Constitution, public treaties, and the laws oblige the President to regard Texas as an independent state, and its territory as no part of the territory of Mexico.

Texas had been an independent state, with an organized government, defying the power of Mexico to overthrow or reconquer her, for more than ten years before Mexico commenced the present war against the United States. Texas had given such evidence to the world of her ability to maintain her separate existence as an independent nation that she had been formally recognized as such not only by the United States, but by several of the principal powers of Europe. These powers had entered into treaties of amity, commerce, and navigation with her. They had received and accredited her ministers and other diplomatic agents at their respective courts, and they had commissioned ministers and diplomatic agents on their part to the Government of Texas. If Mexico, notwithstanding all this and her utter inability to subdue or reconquer Texas, still stubbornly refused to recognize her as an independent nation, she was none the less so on that account. Mexico herself had been recognized as an independent nation by the United States and by other powers many years before Spain, of which before her revolution she had been a colony, would agree to recognize her as such; and yet Mexico was at that time in the estimation of the civilized world, and in fact, none the less an independent power because Spain still claimed her as a colony. If Spain had continued until the present period to assert that Mexico was one of her colonies in rebellion against her, this would not have made her so or changed the fact of her independent existence. Texas at the period of her annexation to the United States bore the same relation to Mexico that Mexico had borne to Spain for many years before Spain acknowledged her independence, with this important difference, that before the annexation of Texas to the United States was consummated Mexico herself, by a formal act of her Government, had acknowledged the independence of Texas as a nation. It is true that in the act of recognition she prescribed a condition which she had no power or authority to impose-that Texas should not annex herself to any other power-but this could not detract in any degree from the recognition which Mexico then made of her actual independence. Upon this plain statement of facts, it is absurd for Mexico to allege as a pretext for commencing hostilities against the United States that Texas is still a part of her territory.

But there are those who, conceding all this to be true, assume the ground that the true western boundary of Texas is the Nueces instead of the Rio Grande, and that therefore in marching our Army to the east bank of the latter river we passed the Texan line and invaded the territory of Mexico. A simple statement of facts known to exist will conclusively refute such an assumption. Texas, as ceded to the United States by France in 1803, has been always claimed as extending west to the Rio Grande or Rio Bravo. This fact is established by the authority of our most eminent statesmen at a period when the question was as well, if not better, understood than it is at present. During Mr. Jefferson's Administration Messrs. Monroe and Pinckney, who had been sent on a special mission to Madrid, charged among other things with the adjustment of boundary between the two countries, in a note addressed to the Spanish minister of foreign affairs under date of the 28th of January, 1805, assert that the boundaries of Louisiana, as ceded to the United States by France, "are the river Perdido on the east and the river Bravo on the west," and they add that "the facts and principles which justify this conclusion are so satisfactory to our Government as to convince it that the United States have not a better right to the island of New Orleans under the cession referred to than they have to the whole district of territory which is above described." Down to the conclusion of the Florida treaty, in February, 1819, by which this territory was ceded to Spain, the United States asserted and maintained their territorial rights to this extent. In the month of June, 1818, during Mr. Monroe's Administration, information having been received that a number of foreign adventurers had landed at Galveston with the avowed purpose of forming a settlement in that vicinity, a special messenger was dispatched by the Government of the United States with instructions from the Secretary of State to warn them to desist, should they be found there, "or any other place north of the Rio Bravo, and within the territory claimed by the United States." He was instructed, should they be found in the country north of that river, to make known to them "the surprise with which the President has seen possession thus taken, without authority from the United States, of a place within their territorial limits, and upon which no lawful settlement can be made without their sanction." He was instructed to call upon them to "avow under what national authority they profess to act," and to give them due warning "that the place is within the United States, who will suffer no permanent settlement to be made there under any authority other than their own." As late as the 8th of July, 1842, the Secretary of State of the United States, in a note addressed to our minister in Mexico, maintains that by the Florida treaty of 1819 the territory as far west as the Rio Grande was confirmed to Spain. In that note he states that-

By the treaty of the 22d of February, 1819, between the United States and Spain, the Sabine was adopted as the line of boundary between the two powers. Up to that period no considerable colonization had been effected in Texas; but the territory between the Sabine and the Rio Grande being confirmed to Spain by the treaty, applications were made to that power for grants of land, and such grants or permissions of settlement were in fact made by the Spanish authorities in favor of citizens of the United States proposing to emigrate to Texas in numerous families before the declaration of independence by Mexico.

The Texas which was ceded to Spain by the Florida treaty of 1819 embraced all the country now claimed by the State of Texas between the Nueces and the Rio Grande. The Republic of Texas always claimed this river as her western boundary, and in her treaty made with Santa Anna in May, 1836, he recognized it as such. By the constitution which Texas adopted in March, 1836, senatorial and representative districts were organized extending west of the Nueces. The Congress of Texas on the 19th of December, 1836, passed "An act to define the boundaries of the Republic of Texas," in which they declared the Rio Grande from its mouth to its source to be their boundary, and by the said act they extended their "civil and political jurisdiction" over the country up to that boundary. During a period of more than nine years which intervened between the adoption of her constitution and her annexation as one of the States of our Union Texas asserted and exercised many acts of sovereignty and jurisdiction over the territory and inhabitants west of the Nueces. She organized and defined the limits of counties extending to the Rio Grande; she established courts of justice and extended her judicial system over the territory; she established a custom-house and collected duties, and also post-offices and post-roads, in it; she established a land office and issued numerous grants for land within its limits; a senator and a representative residing in it were elected to the Congress of the Republic and served as such before the act of annexation took place. In both the Congress and convention of Texas which gave their assent to the terms of annexation to the United States proposed by our Congress were representatives residing west of the Nueces, who took part in the act of annexation itself. This was the Texas which by the act of our Congress of the 29th of December, 1845, was admitted as one of the States of our Union. That the Congress of the United States understood the State of Texas which they admitted into the Union to extend beyond the Nueces is apparent from the fact that on the 31st of December, 1845, only two days after the act of admission, they passed a law "to establish a collection district in the State of Texas," by which they created a port of delivery at Corpus Christi, situated west of the Nueces, and being the same point at which the Texas custom-house under the laws of that Republic had been located, and directed that a surveyor to collect the revenue should be appointed for that port by the President, by and with the advice and consent of the Senate. A surveyor was accordingly nominated, and confirmed by the Senate, and has been ever since in the performance of his duties. All these acts of the Republic of Texas and of our Congress preceded the orders for the advance of our Army to the east bank of the Rio Grande. Subsequently Congress passed an act "establishing certain post routes" extending west of the Nueces. The country west of that river now constitutes a part of one of the Congressional districts of Texas and is represented in the House of Representatives. The Senators from that State were chosen by a legislature in which the country west of that river was represented. In view of all these facts it is difficult to conceive upon what ground it can be maintained that in occupying the country west of the Nueces with our Army, with a view solely to its security and defense, we invaded the territory of Mexico. But it would have been still more difficult to justify the Executive, whose duty it is to see that the laws be faithfully executed, if in the face of all these proceedings, both of the Congress of Texas and of the United States, he had assumed the responsibility of yielding up the territory west of the Nueces to Mexico or of refusing to protect and defend this territory and its inhabitants, including Corpus Christi as well as the remainder of Texas, against the threatened Mexican invasion.

But Mexico herself has never placed the war which she has waged upon the ground that our Army occupied the intermediate territory between the Nueces and the Rio Grande. Her refuted pretension that Texas was not in fact an independent state, but a rebellious province, was obstinately persevered in, and her avowed purpose in commencing a war with the United States was to reconquer Texas and to restore Mexican authority over the whole territory-not to the Nueces only, but to the Sabine. In view of the proclaimed menaces of Mexico to this effect, I deemed it my duty, as a measure of precaution and defense, to order our Army to occupy a position on our frontier as a military post, from which our troops could best resist and repel any attempted invasion which Mexico might make. Our Army had occupied a position at Corpus Christi, west of the Nueces, as early as August, 1845, without complaint from any quarter. Had the Nueces been regarded as the true western boundary of Texas, that boundary had been passed by our Army many months before it advanced to the eastern bank of the Rio Grande. In my annual message of December last I informed Congress that upon the invitation of both the Congress and convention of Texas I had deemed it proper to order a strong squadron to the coasts of Mexico and to concentrate an efficient military force on the western frontier of Texas to protect and defend the inhabitants against the menaced invasion of Mexico. In that message I informed Congress that the moment the terms of annexation offered by the United States were accepted by Texas the latter became so far a part of our own country as to make it our duty to afford such protection and defense, and that for that purpose our squadron had been ordered to the Gulf and our Army to take a "position between the Nueces and the Del Norte" or Rio Grande and to "repel any invasion of the Texan territory which might be attempted by the Mexican forces."

It was deemed proper to issue this order, because soon after the President of Texas, in April, 1845, had issued his proclamation convening the Congress of that Republic for the purpose of submitting to that body the terms of annexation proposed by the United States the Government of Mexico made serious threats of invading the Texan territory. These threats became more imposing as it became more apparent in the progress of the question that the people of Texas would decide in favor of accepting the terms of annexation, and finally they had assumed such a formidable character as induced both the Congress and convention of Texas to request that a military force should be sent by the United States into her territory for the purpose of protecting and defending her against the threatened invasion. It would have been a violation of good faith toward the people of Texas to have refused to afford the aid which they desired against a threatened invasion to which they had been exposed by their free determination to annex themselves to our Union in compliance with the overture made to them by the joint resolution of our Congress. Accordingly, a portion of the Army was ordered to advance into Texas. Corpus Christi was the position selected by General Taylor. He encamped at that place in August, 1845, and the Army remained in that position until the 11th of March, 1846, when it moved westward, and on the 28th of that month reached the east bank of the Rio Grande opposite to Matamoras. This movement was made in pursuance of orders from the War

Department, issued on the 13th of January, 1846. Before these orders were issued the dispatch of our minister in Mexico transmitting the decision of the council of government of Mexico advising that he should not be received, and also the dispatch of our consul residing in the City of Mexico, the former bearing date on the 17th and the latter on the 18th of December, 1845, copies of both of which accompanied my message to Congress of the 11th of May last, were received at the Department of State. These communications rendered it highly probable, if not absolutely certain, that our minister would not be received by the Government of General Herrera. It was also well known that but little hope could be entertained of a different result from General Paredes in case the revolutionary movement which he was prosecuting should prove successful, as was highly probable. The partisans of Paredes, as our minister in the dispatch referred to states, breathed the fiercest hostility against the United States, denounced the proposed negotiation as treason, and openly called upon the troops and the people to put down the Government of Herrera by force. The reconquest of Texas and war with the United States were openly threatened. These were the circumstances existing when it was deemed proper to order the Army under the command of General Taylor to advance to the western frontier of Texas and occupy a position on or near the Rio Grande.

The apprehensions of a contemplated Mexican invasion have been since fully justified by the event. The determination of Mexico to rush into hostilities with the United States was afterwards manifested from the whole tenor of the note of the Mexican minister of foreign affairs to our minister bearing date on the 12th of March, 1846. Paredes had then revolutionized the Government, and his minister, after referring to the resolution for the annexation of Texas which had been adopted by our Congress in March, 1845, proceeds to declare that-

A fact such as this, or, to speak with greater exactness, so notable an act of usurpation, created an imperious necessity that Mexico, for her own honor, should repel it with proper firmness and dignity. The supreme Government had beforehand declared that it would look upon such an act as a casus belli, and as a consequence of this declaration negotiation was by its very nature at an end, and war was the only recourse of the Mexican Government.

It appears also that on the 4th of April following General Paredes, through his minister of war, issued orders to the Mexican general in command on the Texan frontier to "attack" our Army "by every means which war permits." To this General Paredes had been pledged to the army and people of Mexico during the military revolution which had brought him into power. On the 18th of April, 1846, General Paredes addressed a letter to the commander on that frontier in which he stated to him: "At the present date I suppose you, at the head of that valiant army, either fighting already or preparing for the operations of a campaign;" and, "Supposing you already on the theater of operations and with all the forces assembled, it is indispensable that hostilities be commenced, yourself taking the initiative against the enemy."

The movement of our Army to the Rio Grande was made by the commanding general under positive orders to abstain from all aggressive acts toward Mexico or Mexican citizens, and to regard the relations between the two countries as peaceful unless Mexico should declare war or commit acts of hostility indicative of a state of war, and these orders he faithfully executed. Whilst occupying his position on the east bank of the Rio Grande, within the limits of Texas, then recently admitted as one of the States of our Union, the commanding general of the Mexican forces, who, in pursuance of the orders of his Government, had collected a large army on the opposite shore of the Rio Grande, crossed the river, invaded our territory, and commenced hostilities by attacking our forces. Thus, after all the injuries which we had received and borne from Mexico, and after she had insultingly rejected a minister sent to her on a mission of peace, and whom she had solemnly agreed to receive, she consummated her long course of outrage against our country by commencing an offensive war and shedding the blood of our citizens on our own soil.

The United States never attempted to acquire Texas by conquest. On the contrary, at an early period after the people of Texas had achieved their independence they sought to be annexed to the United States. At a general election in September, 1836, they decided with great unanimity in favor of "annexation," and in November following the Congress of the Republic authorized the appointment of a minister to bear their request to this Government. This Government, however, having remained neutral between Texas and Mexico during the war between them, and considering it due to the honor of our country and our fair fame among the nations of the earth that we should not at this early period consent to annexation, nor until it should be manifest to the whole world that the reconquest of Texas by Mexico was impossible, refused to accede to the overtures made by Texas. On the 12th of April, 1844, after more than seven years had elapsed since Texas had established her independence, a treaty was concluded for the annexation of that Republic to the United States, which was rejected by the Senate. Finally, on the 1st of March, 1845, Congress passed a joint resolution for annexing her to the United States upon certain preliminary conditions to which her assent was required. The solemnities which characterized the deliberations and conduct of the Government and people of Texas on the deeply interesting questions presented by these resolutions are known to the world. The Congress, the Executive, and the people of Texas, in a convention elected for that purpose, accepted with great unanimity the proposed terms of annexation, and thus consummated on her part the great act of restoring to our Federal Union a vast territory which had been ceded to Spain by the Florida treaty more than a quarter of a century before.

After the joint resolution for the annexation of Texas to the United States had been passed by our Congress the Mexican minister at Washington addressed a note to the Secretary of State, bearing date on the 6th of March, 1845, protesting against it as "an act of aggression the most unjust which can be found recorded in the annals of modern history, namely, that of despoiling a friendly nation like Mexico of a considerable portion of her territory," and protesting against the resolution of annexation as being an act "whereby the Province of Texas, an integral portion of the Mexican territory, is agreed and admitted into the American Union;" and he announced that as a consequence his mission to the United States had terminated, and demanded his passports, which were granted. It was upon the absurd pretext, made by Mexico (herself indebted for her independence to a successful revolution), that the Republic of Texas still continued to be, notwithstanding all that had passed, a Province of Mexico that this step was taken by the Mexican minister.

Every honorable effort has been used by me to avoid the war which followed, but all have proved vain. All our attempts to preserve peace have been met by insult and resistance on the part of Mexico. My efforts to this end commenced in the note of the Secretary of State of the 10th of March, 1845, in answer to that of the Mexican minister. Whilst declining to reopen a discussion which had already been exhausted, and proving again what was known to the whole world, that Texas had long since achieved her independence, the Secretary of State expressed the regret of this Government that Mexico should have taken offense at the resolution of annexation passed by Congress, and gave assurance that our "most strenuous efforts shall be devoted to the amicable adjustment of every cause of complaint between the two Governments and to the cultivation of the kindest and most friendly relations between the sister Republics." That I have acted in the spirit of this assurance will appear from the events which have since occurred. Notwithstanding Mexico had abruptly terminated all diplomatic intercourse with the United States, and ought, therefore, to have been the first to ask for its resumption, yet, waiving all ceremony, I embraced the earliest favorable opportunity "to ascertain from the Mexican Government whether they would receive an envoy from the United States intrusted with full power to adjust all the questions in dispute between the two Governments." In September, 1845, I believed the propitious moment for such an overture had arrived. Texas, by the enthusiastic and almost unanimous will of her people, had pronounced in favor of annexation. Mexico herself had agreed to acknowledge the independence of Texas, subject to a condition, it is true, which she had no right to impose and no power to enforce. The last lingering hope of Mexico, if she still could have retained any, that Texas would ever again become one of her Provinces, must have been abandoned.

The consul of the United States at the City of Mexico was therefore instructed by the Secretary of State on the 15th of September, 1845, to make the inquiry of the Mexican Government. The inquiry was made, and on the 15th of October, 1845, the minister of foreign affairs of the Mexican Government, in a note addressed to our consul, gave a favorable response, requesting at the same time that our naval force might be withdrawn from Vera Cruz while negotiations should be pending. Upon the receipt of this note our naval force was promptly withdrawn from Vera Cruz. A minister was immediately appointed, and departed to Mexico. Everything bore a promising aspect for a speedy and peaceful adjustment of all our difficulties. At the date of my annual message to Congress in December last no doubt was entertained but that he would be received by the Mexican Government, and the hope was cherished that all cause of misunderstanding between the two countries would be speedily removed. In the confident hope that such would be the result of his mission, I informed Congress that I forbore at that time to "recommend such ulterior measures of redress for the wrongs and injuries we had so long borne as it would have been proper to make had no such negotiation been instituted." To my surprise and regret the Mexican Government, though solemnly pledged to do so, upon the arrival of our minister in Mexico refused to receive and accredit him. When he reached Vera Cruz, on the 30th of November, 1845, he found that the aspect of affairs had undergone an unhappy change. The Government of General Herrera, who was at that time President of the Republic, was tottering to its fall. General Paredes, a military leader, had manifested his determination to overthrow the Government of Herrera by a military revolution, and one of the principal means which he employed to effect his purpose and render the Government of Herrera odious to the army and people of Mexico was by loudly condemning its determination to receive a minister of peace from the United States, alleging that it was the intention of Herrera, by a treaty with the United States, to dismember the territory of Mexico by ceding away the department of Texas. The Government of

Herrera is believed to have been well disposed to a pacific adjustment of existing difficulties, but probably alarmed for its own security, and in order to ward off the danger of the revolution led by Paredes, violated its solemn agreement and refused to receive or accredit our minister; and this although informed that he had been invested with full power to adjust all questions in dispute between the two Governments. Among the frivolous pretexts for this refusal, the principal one was that our minister had not gone upon a special mission confined to the question of Texas alone, leaving all the outrages upon our flag and our citizens unredressed. The Mexican Government well knew that both our national honor and the protection due to our citizens imperatively required that the two questions of boundary and indemnity should be treated of together, as naturally and inseparably blended, and they ought to have seen that this course was best calculated to enable the United States to extend to them the most liberal justice. On the 30th of December, 1845, General Herrera resigned the Presidency and yielded up the Government to General Paredes without a struggle. Thus a revolution was accomplished solely by the army commanded by Paredes, and the supreme power in Mexico passed into the hands of a military usurper who was known to be bitterly hostile to the United States.

Although the prospect of a pacific adjustment with the new Government was unpromising from the known hostility of its head to the United States, yet, determined that nothing should be left undone on our part to restore friendly relations between the two countries, our minister was instructed to present his credentials to the new Government and ask to be accredited by it in the diplomatic character in which he had been commissioned. These instructions he executed by his note of the 1st of March, 1846, addressed to the Mexican minister of foreign affairs, but his request was insultingly refused by that minister in his answer of the 12th of the same month. No alternative remained for our minister but to demand his passports and return to the United States.

Thus was the extraordinary spectacle presented to the civilized world of a Government, in violation of its own express agreement, having twice rejected a minister of peace invested with full powers to adjust all the existing differences between the two countries in a manner just and honorable to both. I am not aware that modern history presents a parallel case in which in time of peace one nation has refused even to hear propositions from another for terminating existing difficulties between them. Scarcely a hope of adjusting our difficulties, even at a remote day, or of preserving peace with Mexico, could be cherished while Paredes remained at the head of the Government. He had acquired the supreme power by a military revolution and upon the most solemn pledges to wage war against the United States and to reconquer Texas, which he claimed as a revolted province of Mexico. He had denounced as guilty of treason all those Mexicans who considered Texas as no longer constituting a part of the territory of Mexico and who were friendly to the cause of peace. The duration of the war which he waged against the United States was indefinite, because the end which he proposed of the reconquest of Texas was hopeless. Besides, there was good reason to believe from all his conduct that it was his intention to convert the Republic of Mexico into a monarchy and to call a foreign European prince to the throne. Preparatory to this end, he had during his short rule destroyed the liberty of the press, tolerating that portion of it only which openly advocated the establishment of a monarchy. The better to secure the success of his ultimate designs, he had by an arbitrary decree convoked a Congress, not to be elected by the free voice of the people, but to be chosen in a manner to make them subservient to his will and to give him absolute control over their deliberations.

Under all these circumstances it was believed that any revolution in Mexico founded upon opposition to the ambitious projects of Paredes would tend to promote the cause of peace as well as prevent any attempted European interference in the affairs of the North American continent, both objects of deep interest to the United States. Any such foreign interference, if attempted, must have been resisted by the United States. My views upon that subject were fully communicated to Congress in my last annual message. In any event, it was certain that no change whatever in the Government of Mexico which would deprive Paredes of power could be for the worse so far as the United States were concerned, while it was highly probable that any change must be for the better. This was the state of affairs existing when Congress, on the 13th of May last, recognized the existence of the war which had been commenced by the Government of Paredes; and it became an object of much importance, with a view to a speedy settlement of our difficulties and the restoration of an honorable peace, that Paredes should not retain power in Mexico.

Before that time there were symptoms of a revolution in Mexico, favored, as it was understood to be, by the more liberal party, and especially by those who were opposed to foreign interference and to the monarchical form of government. Santa Anna was then in exile in Havana, having been expelled from power and banished from his country by a revolution which occurred in December, 1844; but it was known that he had still a considerable party in his favor in Mexico. It was also equally well known that no vigilance which could be exerted by our squadron would in all probability have prevented him from effecting a landing somewhere on the extensive Gulf coast of Mexico if he desired to return to his country. He had openly professed an entire change of policy, had expressed his regret that he had subverted the federal constitution of 1824, and avowed that he was now in favor of its restoration. He had publicly declared his hostility, in strongest terms, to the establishment of a monarchy and to European interference in the affairs of his country. Information to this effect had been received, from sources believed to be reliable, at the date of the recognition of the existence of the war by Congress, and was afterwards fully confirmed by the receipt of the dispatch of our consul in the City of Mexico, with the accompanying documents, which are herewith transmitted. Besides, it was reasonable to suppose that he must see the ruinous consequences to Mexico of a war with the United States, and that it would be his interest to favor peace.

It was under these circumstances and upon these considerations that it was deemed expedient not to obstruct his return to Mexico should he attempt to do so. Our object was the restoration of peace, and, with that view, no reason was perceived why we should take part with Paredes and aid him by means of our blockade in preventing the return of his rival to Mexico. On the contrary, it was believed that the intestine divisions which ordinary sagacity could not but anticipate as the fruit of Santa Anna's return to Mexico, and his contest with Paredes, might strongly tend to produce a disposition with both parties to restore and preserve peace with the United States. Paredes was a soldier by profession and a monarchist in principle. He had but recently before been successful in a military revolution, by which he had obtained power. He was the sworn enemy of the United States, with which he had involved his country in the existing war. Santa Anna had been expelled from power by the army, was known to be in open hostility to Paredes, and publicly pledged against foreign intervention and the restoration of monarchy in Mexico. In view of these facts and circumstances it was that when orders were issued to the commander of our naval forces in the Gulf, on the 13th day of May last, the same day on which the existence of the war was recognized by Congress, to place the coasts of Mexico under blockade, he was directed not to obstruct the passage of Santa Anna to Mexico should he attempt to return.

A revolution took place in Mexico in the early part of August following, by which the power of Paredes was overthrown, and he has since been banished from the country, and is now in exile. Shortly afterwards Santa Anna returned. It remains to be seen whether his return may not yet prove to be favorable to a pacific adjustment of the existing difficulties, it being manifestly his interest not to persevere in the prosecution of a war commenced by Paredes to accomplish a purpose so absurd as the reconquest of Texas to the Sabine. Had Paredes remained in power, it is morally certain that any pacific adjustment would have been hopeless.

Upon the commencement of hostilities by Mexico against the United States the indignant spirit of the nation was at once aroused. Congress promptly responded to the expectations of the country, and by the act of the 13th of May last recognized the fact that war existed, by the act of Mexico, between the United States and that Republic, and granted the means necessary for its vigorous prosecution. Being involved in a war thus commenced by Mexico, and for the justice of which on our part we may confidently appeal to the whole world, I resolved to prosecute it with the utmost vigor. Accordingly the ports of Mexico on the Gulf and on the Pacific have been placed under blockade and her territory invaded at several important points. The reports from the Departments of War and of the Navy will inform you more in detail of the measures adopted in the emergency in which our country was placed and of the gratifying results which have been accomplished.

The various columns of the Army have performed their duty under great disadvantages with the most distinguished skill and courage. The victories of Palo Alto and Resaca de la Palma and of Monterey, won against greatly superior numbers and against most decided advantages in other respects on the part of the enemy, were brilliant in their execution, and entitle our brave officers and soldiers to the grateful thanks of their country. The nation deplores the loss of the brave officers and men who have gallantly fallen while vindicating and defending their country's rights and honor.

It is a subject of pride and satisfaction that our volunteer citizen soldiers, who so promptly responded to their country's call, with an experience of the discipline of a camp of only a few weeks, have borne their part in the hard-fought battle of Monterey with a constancy and courage equal to that of veteran troops and worthy of the highest admiration. The privations of long marches through the enemy's country and through a wilderness have been borne without a murmur. By rapid movements the Province of New Mexico, with Santa Fe, its capital, has been captured without bloodshed. The Navy has cooperated with the Army and rendered important services; if not so brilliant, it is because the enemy had no force to meet them on their own element and because of the defenses which nature has interposed in the difficulties of the navigation on the Mexican coast. Our squadron in the Pacific, with the cooperation of a gallant officer of the Army and a small force hastily collected in that distant country, has acquired bloodless possession of the Californias, and the American flag has been raised at every important point in that Province.

I congratulate you on the success which has thus attended our military and naval operations. In less than seven months after Mexico commenced hostilities, at a time selected by herself, we have taken possession of many of her principal ports, driven back and pursued her invading army, and acquired military possession of the Mexican Provinces of New Mexico, New Leon, Coahuila, Tamaulipas, and the Californias, a territory larger in extent than that embraced in the original thirteen States of the Union, inhabited by a considerable population, and much of it more than 1,000 miles from the points at which we had to collect our forces and commence our movements. By the blockade the import and export trade of the enemy has been cut off. Well may the American people be proud of the energy and gallantry of our regular and volunteer officers and soldiers. The events of these few months afford a gratifying proof that our country can under any emergency confidently rely for the maintenance of her honor and the defense of her rights on an effective force, ready at all times voluntarily to relinquish the comforts of home for the perils and privations of the camp. And though such a force may be for the time expensive, it is in the end economical, as the ability to command it removes the necessity of employing a large standing army in time of peace, and proves that our people love their institutions and are ever ready to defend and protect them.

While the war was in a course of vigorous and successful prosecution, being still anxious to arrest its evils, and considering that after the brilliant victories of our arms on the 8th and 9th of May last the national honor could not be compromitted by it, another overture was made to Mexico, by my direction, on the 27th of July last to terminate hostilities by a peace just and honorable to both countries. On the 31st of August following the Mexican Government declined to accept this friendly overture, but referred it to the decision of a Mexican Congress to be assembled in the early part of the present month. I communicate to you herewith a copy of the letter of the Secretary of State proposing to reopen negotiations, of the answer of the Mexican Government, and of the reply thereto of the Secretary of State,

The war will continue to be prosecuted with vigor as the best means of securing peace. It is hoped that the decision of the Mexican Congress, to which our last overture has been referred, may result in a speedy and honorable peace. With our experience, however, of the unreasonable course of the Mexican authorities, it is the part of wisdom not to relax in the energy of our military operations until the result is made known. In this view it is deemed important to hold military possession of all the Provinces which have been taken until a definitive treaty of peace shall have been concluded and ratified by the two countries.

The war has not been waged with a view to conquest, but, having been commenced by Mexico, it has been carried into the enemy's country and will be vigorously prosecuted there with a view to obtain an honorable peace, and thereby secure ample indemnity for the expenses of the war, as well as to our much-injured citizens, who hold large pecuniary demands against Mexico.

By the laws of nations a conquered country is subject to be governed by the conqueror during his military possession and until there is either a treaty of peace or he shall voluntarily withdraw from it. The old civil government being necessarily superseded, it is the right and duty of the conqueror to secure his conquest and to provide for the maintenance of civil order and the rights of the inhabitants. This right has been exercised and this duty performed by our military and naval commanders by the establishment of temporary governments in some of the conquered Provinces of Mexico, assimilating them as far as practicable to the free institutions of our own country. In the Provinces of New Mexico and of the Californias little, if any, further resistance is apprehended from the inhabitants to the temporary governments which have thus, from the necessity of the case and according to the laws of war, been established. It may be proper to provide for the security of these important conquests by making an adequate appropriation for the purpose of erecting fortifications and defraying the expenses necessarily incident to the maintenance of our possession and authority over them.

Near the close of your last session, for reasons communicated to Congress, I deemed it important as a measure for securing a speedy peace with Mexico, that a sum of money should be appropriated and placed in the power of the Executive, similar to that which had been made upon two former occasions during the Administration of President Jefferson.

On the 26th of February, 1803, an appropriation of $2,000.000 was made and placed at the disposal of the President. Its object is well known. It was at that time in contemplation to acquire Louisiana from France, and it was intended to be applied as a part of the consideration which might be paid for that territory. On the 13th of February, 1806, the same sum was in like manner appropriated, with a view to the purchase of the Floridas from Spain. These appropriations were made to facilitate negotiations and as a means to enable the President to accomplish the important objects in view. Though it did not become necessary for the President to use these appropriations, yet a state of things might have arisen in which it would have been highly important for him to do so, and the wisdom of making them can not be doubted. It is believed that the measure recommended at your last session met with the approbation of decided majorities in both Houses of Congress. Indeed, in different forms, a bill making an appropriation of $2,000,000 passed each House, and it is much to be regretted that it did not become a law. The reasons which induced me to recommend the measure at that time still exist, and I again submit the subject for your consideration and suggest the importance of early action upon it. Should the appropriation be made and be not needed, it will remain in the Treasury; should it be deemed proper to apply it in whole or in part, it will be accounted for as other public expenditures.

Immediately after Congress had recognized the existence of the war with Mexico my attention was directed to the danger that privateers might be fitted out in the ports of Cuba and Porto Rico to prey upon the commerce of the United States, and I invited the special attention of the Spanish Government to the fourteenth article of our treaty with that power of the 27th of October, 1795, under which the citizens and subjects of either nation who shall take commissions or letters of marque to act as privateers against the other "shall be punished as pirates."

It affords me pleasure to inform you that I have received assurances from the Spanish Government that this article of the treaty shall be faithfully observed on its part. Orders for this purpose were immediately transmitted from that Government to the authorities of Cuba and Porto Rico to exert their utmost vigilance in preventing any attempts to fit out privateers in those islands against the United States. From the good faith of Spain I am fully satisfied that this treaty will be executed in its spirit as well as its letter, whilst the United States will on their part faithfully perform all the obligations which it imposes on them.

Information has been recently received at the Department of State that the Mexican Government has sent to Havana blank commissions to privateers and blank certificates of naturalization signed by General Salas, the present head of the Mexican Government. There is also reason to apprehend that similar documents have been transmitted to other parts of the world. Copies of these papers, in translation, are herewith transmitted.

As the preliminaries required by the practice of civilized nations for commissioning privateers and regulating their conduct appear not to have been observed, and as these commissions are in blank, to be filled up with the names of citizens and subjects of all nations who may be willing to purchase them, the whole proceeding can only be construed as an invitation to all the freebooters upon earth who are willing to pay for the privilege to cruise against American commerce. It will be for our courts of justice to decide whether under such circumstances these Mexican letters of marque and reprisal shall protect those who accept them, and commit robberies upon the high seas under their authority, from the pains and penalties of piracy.

If the certificates of naturalization thus granted be intended by Mexico to shield Spanish subjects from the guilt and punishment of pirates under our treaty with Spain, they will certainly prove unavailing. Such a subterfuge would be but a weak device to defeat the provisions of a solemn treaty.

I recommend that Congress should immediately provide by law for the trial and punishment as pirates of Spanish subjects who, escaping the vigilance of their Government, shall be found guilty of privateering against the United States. I do not apprehend serious danger from these privateers. Our Navy will be constantly on the alert to protect our commerce. Besides, in case prizes should be made of American vessels, the utmost vigilance will be exerted by our blockading squadron to prevent the captors from taking them into Mexican ports, and it is not apprehended that any nation will violate its neutrality by suffering such prizes to be condemned and sold within its jurisdiction.

I recommend that Congress should immediately provide by law for granting letters of marque and reprisal against vessels under the Mexican flag. It is true that there are but few, if any, commercial vessels of Mexico upon the high seas, and it is therefore not probable that many American privateers would be fitted out in case a law should pass authorizing this mode of warfare. It is, notwithstanding, certain that such privateers may render good service to the commercial interests of the country by recapturing our merchant ships should any be taken by armed vessels under the Mexican flag, as well as by capturing these vessels themselves. Every means within our power should be rendered available for the protection of our commerce.

The annual report of the Secretary of the Treasury will exhibit a detailed statement of the condition of the finances. The imports for the fiscal year ending on the 30th of June last were of the value of $121,691,797, of which the amount exported was $11,346,623, leaving the amount retained in the country for domestic consumption $110,345,174. The value of the exports for the same period was $113,488,516, of which $102,141,893 consisted of domestic productions and $11,346,623 of foreign articles.

The receipts into the Treasury for the same year were $29,499,247.06, of which there was derived from customs $26,712,667.87, from the sales of public lands $2,694,452.48, and from incidental and miscellaneous sources $92,126.71. The expenditures for the same period were $28,031,114.20, and the balance in the Treasury on the 1st day of July last was $9,126,439. 08.

The amount of the public debt, including Treasury notes, on the 1st of the present month was $24,256,494.60, of which the sum of $17,788,799.62 was outstanding on the 4th of March, 1845, leaving the amount incurred since that time $6,467,694.98.

In order to prosecute the war with Mexico with vigor and energy, as the best means of bringing it to a speedy and honorable termination, a further loan will be necessary to meet the expenditures for the present and the next fiscal year. If the war should be continued until the 30th of June, 1848, being the end of the next fiscal year, it is estimated that an additional loan of $23,000,000 will be required. This estimate is made upon the assumption that it will be necessary to retain constantly in the Treasury $4,000,000 to guard against contingencies. If such surplus were not required to be retained, then a loan of $19,000,000 would be sufficient. If, however, Congress should at the present session impose a revenue duty on the principal articles now embraced in the free list, it is estimated that an additional annual revenue of about two millions and a half, amounting, it is estimated, on the 30th of June, 1848, to $4,000,000, would be derived from that source, and the loan required would be reduced by that amount. It is estimated also that should Congress graduate and reduce the price of such of the public lands as have been long in the market the additional revenue derived from that source would be annually, for several years to come, between half a million and a million dollars; and the loan required may be reduced by that amount also. Should these measures be adopted, the loan required would not probably exceed $18,000,000 or $19,000,000, leaving in the Treasury a constant surplus of $4,000,000. The loan proposed, it is estimated, will be sufficient to cover the necessary expenditures both for the war and for all other purposes up to the 30th of June, 1848, and an amount of this loan not exceeding one-half may be required during the present fiscal year, and the greater part of the remainder during the first half of the fiscal year succeeding.

In order that timely notice may be given and proper measures taken to effect the loan, or such portion of it as may be required, it is important that the authority of Congress to make it be given at an early period of your present session. It is suggested that the loan should be contracted for a period of twenty years, with authority to purchase the stock and pay it off at an earlier period at its market value out of any surplus which may at any time be in the Treasury applicable to that purpose. After the establishment of peace with Mexico, it is supposed that a considerable surplus will exist, and that the debt may be extinguished in a much shorter period than that for which it may be contracted. The period of twenty years, as that for which the proposed loan may be contracted, in preference to a shorter period, is suggested, because all experience, both at home and abroad, has shown that loans are effected upon much better terms upon long time than when they are reimbursable at short dates.

Necessary as this measure is to sustain the honor and the interests of the country engaged in a foreign war, it is not doubted but that Congress will promptly authorize it.

The balance in the Treasury on the 1st July last exceeded $9,000,000, notwithstanding considerable expenditures had been made for the war during the months of May and June preceding. But for the war the whole public debt could and would have been extinguished within a short period; and it was a part of my settled policy to do so, and thus relieve the people from its burden and place the Government in a position which would enable it to reduce the public expenditures to that economical standard which is most consistent with the general welfare and the pure and wholesome progress of our institutions.

Among our just causes of complaint against Mexico arising out of her refusal to treat for peace, as well before as since the war so unjustly commenced on her part, are the extraordinary expenditures in which we have been involved. Justice to our own people will make it proper that Mexico should be held responsible for these expenditures.

Economy in the public expenditures is at all times a high duty which all public functionaries of the Government owe to the people. This duty becomes the more imperative in a period of war, when large and extraordinary expenditures become unavoidable. During the existence of the war with Mexico all our resources should be husbanded, and no appropriations made except such as are absolutely necessary for its vigorous prosecution and the due administration of the Government. Objects of appropriation which in peace may be deemed useful or proper, but which are not indispensable for the public service, may when the country is engaged in a foreign war be well postponed to a future period. By the observance of this policy at your present session large amounts may be saved to the Treasury and be applied to objects of pressing and urgent necessity, and thus the creation of a corresponding amount of public debt may be avoided.

It is not meant to recommend that the ordinary and necessary appropriations for the support of Government should be withheld; but it is well known that at every session of Congress appropriations are proposed for numerous objects which may or may not be made without materially affecting the public interests, and these it is recommended should not be granted.

The act passed at your last session "reducing the duties on imports" not having gone into operation until the 1st of the present month, there has not been time for its practical effect upon the revenue and the business of the country to be developed. It is not doubted, however, that the just policy which it adopts will add largely to our foreign trade and promote the general prosperity. Although it can not be certainly foreseen what amount of revenue it will yield, it is estimated that it will exceed that produced by the act of 1842, which it superseded. The leading principles established by it are to levy the taxes with a view to raise revenue and to impose them upon the articles imported according to their actual value.

The act of 1842, by the excessive rates of duty which it imposed on many articles, either totally excluded them from importation or greatly reduced the amount imported, and thus diminished instead of producing revenue. By it the taxes were imposed not for the legitimate purpose of raising revenue, but to afford advantages to favored classes at the expense of a large majority of their fellow-citizens. Those employed in agriculture, mechanical pursuits, commerce, and navigation were compelled to contribute from their substance to swell the profits and overgrown wealth of the comparatively few who had invested their capital in manufactures. The taxes were not levied in proportion to the value of the articles upon which they were imposed, but, widely departing from this just rule, the lighter taxes were in many cases levied upon articles of luxury and high price and the heavier taxes on those of necessity and low price, consumed by the great mass of the people. It was a system the inevitable effect of which was to relieve favored classes and the wealthy few from contributing their just proportion for the support of Government, and to lay the burden on the labor of the many engaged in other pursuits than manufactures.

A system so unequal and unjust has been superseded by the existing law, which imposes duties not for the benefit or injury of classes or pursuits, but distributes and, as far as practicable, equalizes the public burdens among all classes and occupations. The favored classes who under the unequal and unjust system which has been repealed have heretofore realized large profits, and many of them amassed large fortunes at the expense of the many who have been made tributary to them, will have no reason to complain if they shall be required to bear their just proportion of the taxes necessary for the support of Government. So far from it, it will be perceived by an examination of the existing law that discriminations in the rates of duty imposed within the revenue principle have been retained in their favor. The incidental aid against foreign competition which they still enjoy gives them an advantage which no other pursuits possess, but of this none others will complain, because the duties levied are necessary for revenue. These revenue duties, including freights and charges, which the importer must pay before he can come in competition with the home manufacturer in our markets, amount on nearly all our leading branches of manufacture to more than one-third of the value of the imported article, and in some cases to almost one-half its value. With such advantages it is not doubted that our domestic manufacturers will continue to prosper, realizing in well-conducted establishments even greater profits than can be derived from any other regular business. Indeed, so far from requiring the protection of even incidental revenue duties, our manufacturers in several leading branches are extending their business, giving evidence of great ingenuity and skill and of their ability to compete, with increased prospect of success, for the open market of the world. Domestic manufactures to the value of several millions of dollars, which can not find a market at home, are annually exported to foreign countries. With such rates of duty as those established by the existing law the system will probably be permanent, and capitalists who are made or shall hereafter make their investments in manufactures will know upon what to rely. The country will be satisfied with these rates, because the advantages which the manufacturers still enjoy result necessarily from the collection of revenue for the support of Government. High protective duties, from their unjust operation upon the masses of the people, can not fail to give rise to extensive dissatisfaction and complaint and to constant efforts to change or repeal them, rendering all investments in manufactures uncertain and precarious. Lower and more permanent rates of duty, at the same time that they will yield to the manufacturer fair and remunerating profits, will secure him against the danger of frequent changes in the system, which can not fail to ruinously affect his interests.

Simultaneously with the relaxation of the restrictive policy by the United States, Great Britain, from whose example we derived the system, has relaxed hers. She has modified her corn laws and reduced many other duties to moderate revenue rates. After ages of experience the statesmen of that country have been constrained by a stern necessity and by a public opinion having its deep foundation in the sufferings and wants of impoverished millions to abandon a system the effect of which was to build up immense fortunes in the hands of the few and to reduce the laboring millions to pauperism and misery. Nearly in the same ratio that labor was depressed capital was increased and concentrated by the British protective policy.

The evils of the system in Great Britain were at length rendered intolerable, and it has been abandoned, but not without a severe struggle on the part of the protected and favored classes to retain the unjust advantages which they have so long enjoyed. It was to be expected that a similar struggle would be made by the same classes in the United States whenever an attempt was made to modify or abolish the same unjust system here. The protective policy had been in operation in the United States for a much shorter period, and its pernicious effects were not, therefore, so clearly perceived and felt. Enough, however, was known of these effects to induce its repeal.

It would be strange if in the face of the example of Great Britain, our principal foreign customer, and of the evils of a system rendered manifest in that country by long and painful experience, and in the face of the immense advantages which under a more liberal commercial policy we are already deriving, and must continue to derive, by supplying her starving population with food, the United States should restore a policy which she has been compelled to abandon, and thus diminish her ability to purchase from us the food and other articles which she so much needs and we so much desire to sell. By the simultaneous abandonment of the protective policy by Great Britain and the United States new and important markets have already been opened for our agricultural and other products, commerce and navigation have received a new impulse, labor and trade have been released from the artificial trammels which have so long fettered them, and to a great extent reciprocity in the exchange of commodities has been introduced at the same time by both countries, and greatly for the benefit of both. Great Britain has been forced by the pressure of circumstances at home to abandon a policy which has been upheld for ages, and to open her markets for our immense surplus of breadstuffs, and it is confidently believed that other powers of Europe will ultimately see the wisdom, if they be not compelled by the pauperism and sufferings of their crowded population, to pursue a similar policy.

Our farmers are more deeply interested in maintaining the just and liberal policy of the existing law than any other class of our citizens. They constitute a large majority of our population, and it is well known that when they prosper all other pursuits prosper also. They have heretofore not only received none of the bounties or favors of Government, but by the unequal operations of the protective policy have been made by the burdens of taxation which it imposed to contribute to the bounties which have enriched others.

When a foreign as well as a home market is opened to them, they must receive, as they are now receiving, increased prices for their products. They will find a readier sale, and at better prices, for their wheat, flour, rice, Indian corn, beef, pork, lard, butter, cheese, and other articles which they produce. The home market alone is inadequate to enable them to dispose of the immense surplus of food and other articles which they are capable of producing, even at the most reduced prices, for the manifest reason that they can not be consumed in the country. The United States can from their immense surplus supply not only the home demand, but the deficiencies of food required by the whole world.

That the reduced production of some of the chief articles of food in Great Britain and other parts of Europe may have contributed to increase the demand for our breadstuffs and provisions is not doubted, but that the great and efficient cause of this increased demand and of increased prices consists in the removal of artificial restrictions heretofore imposed is deemed to be equally certain. That our exports of food, already increased and increasing beyond former example under the more liberal policy which has been adopted, will be still vastly enlarged unless they be checked or prevented by a restoration of the protective policy can not be doubted. That our commercial and navigating interests will be enlarged in a corresponding ratio with the increase of our trade is equally certain, while our manufacturing interests will still be the favored interests of the country and receive the incidental protection afforded them by revenue duties; and more than this they can not justly demand.

In my annual message of December last a tariff of revenue duties based upon the principles of the existing law was recommended, and I have seen no reason to change the opinions then expressed. In view of the probable beneficial effects of that law, I recommend that the policy established by it be maintained. It has but just commenced to operate, and to abandon or modify it without giving it a fair trial would be inexpedient and unwise. Should defects in any of its details be ascertained by actual experience to exist, these may be hereafter corrected; but until such defects shall become manifest the act should be fairly tested.

It is submitted for your consideration whether it may not be proper, as a war measure, to impose revenue duties on some of the articles now embraced in the free list. Should it be deemed proper to impose such duties with a view to raise revenue to meet the expenses of the war with Mexico or to avoid to that extent the creation of a public debt, they may be repealed when the emergency which gave rise to them shall cease to exist, and constitute no part of the permanent policy of the country.

The act of the 6th of August last, "to provide for the better organization of the Treasury and for the collection, safe-keeping, transfer, and disbursement of the public revenue," has been carried into execution as rapidly as the delay necessarily arising out of the appointment of new officers, taking and approving their bonds, and preparing and securing proper places for the safe-keeping of the public money would permit. It is not proposed to depart in any respect from the principles or policy on which this great measure is rounded. There are, however, defects in the details of the measure, developed by its practical operation, which are fully set forth in the report of the Secretary of the Treasury, to which the attention of Congress is invited. These defects would impair to some extent the successful operation of the law at all times, but are especially embarrassing when the country is engaged in a war, when the expenditures are greatly increased, when loans are to be effected and the disbursements are to be made at points many hundred miles distant, in some cases, from any depository, and a large portion of them in a foreign country. The modifications suggested in the report of the Secretary of the Treasury are recommended to your favorable consideration.

In connection with this subject I invite your attention to the importance of establishing a branch of the Mint of the United States at New York. Two-thirds of the revenue derived from customs being collected at that point, the demand for specie to pay the duties will be large, and a branch mint where foreign coin and bullion could be immediately converted into American coin would greatly facilitate the transaction of the public business, enlarge the circulation of gold and silver, and be at the same time a safe depository of the public money.

The importance of graduating and reducing the price of such of the public lands as have been long offered in the market at the minimum rate authorized by existing laws, and remain unsold, induces me again to recommend the subject to your favorable consideration. Many millions of acres of these lands have been offered in the market for more than thirty years and larger quantities for more than ten or twenty years, and, being of an inferior quality, they must remain unsalable for an indefinite period unless the price at which they may be purchased shall be reduced. To place a price upon them above their real value is not only to prevent their sale, and thereby deprive the Treasury of any income from that source, but is unjust to the States in which they lie, because it retards their growth and increase of population, and because they have no power to levy a tax upon them as upon other lands within their limits, held by other proprietors than the United States, for the support of their local governments.

The beneficial effects of the graduation principle have been realized by some of the States owning the lands within their limits in which it has been adopted. They have been demonstrated also by the United States acting as the trustee of the Chickasaw tribe of Indians in the sale of their lands lying within the States of Mississippi and Alabama. The Chickasaw lands, which would not command in the market the minimum price established by the laws of the United States for the sale of their lands, were, in pursuance of the treaty of 1834 with that tribe, subsequently offered for sale at graduated and reduced rates for limited periods. The result was that large quantities of these lands were purchased which would otherwise have remained unsold. The lands were disposed of at their real value, and many persons of limited means were enabled to purchase small tracts, upon which they have settled with their families. That similar results would be produced by the adoption of the graduation policy by the United States in all the States in which they are the owners of large bodies of lands which have been long in the market can not be doubted. It can not be a sound policy to withhold large quantities of the public lands from the use and occupation of our citizens by fixing upon them prices which experience has shown they will not command. On the contrary, it is a wise policy to afford facilities to our citizens to become the owners at low and moderate rates of freeholds of their own instead of being the tenants and dependents of others. If it be apprehended that these lands if reduced in price would be secured in large quantities by speculators or capitalists, the sales may be restricted in limited quantities to actual settlers or persons purchasing for purposes of cultivation.

In my last annual message I submitted for the consideration of Congress the present system of managing the mineral lands of the United States, and recommended that they should be brought into market and sold upon such terms and under such restrictions as Congress might prescribe. By the act of the 11th of July last "the reserved lead mines and contiguous lands in the States of Illinois and Arkansas and Territories of Wisconsin and Iowa" were authorized to be sold. The act is confined in its operation to "lead mines and contiguous lands." A large portion of the public lands, containing copper and other ores, is represented to be very valuable, and I recommend that provision be made authorizing the sale of these lands upon such terms and conditions as from their supposed value may in the judgment of Congress be deemed advisable, having due regard to the interests of such of our citizens as may be located upon them.

It will be important during your present session to establish a Territorial government and to extend the jurisdiction and laws of the United States over the Territory of Oregon. Our laws regulating trade and intercourse with the Indian tribes east of the Rocky Mountains should be extended to the Pacific Ocean; and for the purpose of executing them and preserving friendly relations with the Indian tribes within our limits, an additional number of Indian agencies will be required, and should be authorized by law. The establishment of custom-houses and of post-offices and post-roads and provision for the transportation of the mail on such routes as the public convenience will suggest require legislative authority. It will be proper also to establish a surveyor-general's office in that Territory and to make the necessary provision for surveying the public lands and bringing them into market. As our citizens who now reside in that distant region have been subjected to many hardships, privations, and sacrifices in their emigration, and by their improvements have enhanced the value of the public lands in the neighborhood of their settlements, it is recommended that liberal grants be made to them ot such portions of these lands as they may occupy, and that similar grants or rights of preemption be made to all who may emigrate thither within a limited period, prescribed by law.

The report of the Secretary of War contains detailed information relative to the several branches of the public service connected with that Department. The operations of the Army have been of a satisfactory and highly gratifying character. I recommend to your early and favorable consideration the measures proposed by the Secretary of War for speedily filling up the rank and file of the Regular Army, for its greater efficiency in the field, and for raising an additional force to serve during the war with Mexico.

Embarrassment is likely to arise for want of legal provision authorizing compensation to be made to the agents employed in the several States and Territories to pay the Revolutionary and other pensioners the amounts allowed them by law. Your attention is invited to the recommendations of the Secretary of War on this subject. These agents incur heavy responsibilities and perform important duties, and no reason exists why they should not be placed on the same footing as to compensation with other disbursing officers.

Our relations with the various Indian tribes continue to be of a pacific character. The unhappy dissensions which have existed among the Cherokees for many years past have been healed. Since my last annual message important treaties have been negotiated with some of the tribes, by which the Indian title to large tracts of valuable land within the limits of the States and Territories has been extinguished and arrangements made for removing them to the country west of the Mississippi. Between 3,000 and 4,000 of different tribes have been removed to the country provided for them by treaty stipulations, and arrangements have been made for others to follow.

In our intercourse with the several tribes particular attention has been given to the important subject of education. The number of schools established among them has been increased, and additional means provided not only for teaching them the rudiments of education, but of instructing them in agriculture and the mechanic arts.

I refer you to the report of the Secretary of the Navy for a satisfactory view of the operations of the Department under his charge during the past year. It is gratifying to perceive that while the war with Mexico has rendered it necessary to employ an unusual number of our armed vessels on her coasts, the protection due to our commerce in other quarters of the world has not proved insufficient. No means will be spared to give efficiency to the naval service in the prosecution of the war; and I am happy to know that the officers and men anxiously desire to devote themselves to the service of their country in any enterprise, however difficult of execution.

I recommend to your favorable consideration the proposition to add to each of our foreign squadrons an efficient sea steamer, and, as especially demanding attention, the establishment at Pensacola of the necessary means of repairing and refitting the vessels of the Navy employed in the Gulf of Mexico.

There are other suggestions in the report which deserve and I doubt not will receive your consideration.

The progress and condition of the mail service for the past year are fully presented in the report of the Postmaster-General. The revenue for the year ending on the 30th of June last amounted to $3,487,199, which is $802,642.45 less than that of the preceding year. The payments for that Department during the same time amounted to $4,084,297.22. Of this sum $597,097.80 have been drawn from the Treasury. The disbursements for the year were $236,434.77 less than those of the preceding year. While the disbursements have been thus diminished, the mail facilities have been enlarged by new mail routes of 5,739 miles, an increase of transportation of 1,764,145 miles, and the establishment of 418 new post-offices. Contractors, postmasters, and others engaged in this branch of the service have performed their duties with energy and faithfulness deserving commendation. For many interesting details connected with the operations of this establishment you are referred to the report of the Postmaster-General, and his suggestions for improving its revenues are recommended to your favorable consideration. I repeat the opinion expressed in my last annual message that the business of this Department should be so regulated that the revenues derived from it should be made to equal the expenditures, and it is believed that this may be done by proper modifications of the present laws, as suggested in the report of the Postmaster-General, without changing the present rates of postage.

With full reliance upon the wisdom and patriotism of your deliberations, it will be my duty, as it will be my anxious desire, to cooperate with you in every constitutional effort to promote the welfare and maintain the honor of our common country.

www.ingramcontent.com/pod-product-compliance
Lightning Source LLC
Chambersburg PA
CBHW070843290526
45795CB00002B/959